HOW TO CARE FOR A

SPIDER MONKEY

A COMPLETE GUIDE THEIR HABITAT, MAINTAINANCE, DIET, PET OWNERSHIP, HEALTH CARE, AND MANY MORE INCLUDED

Dr Morris Hart

Copyright© 2024 **Dr Morris Hart**

All rights reserved. No part or part of this book or publication may be reproduced, stored, or transferred in any form by electronic, mechanical, recording, or other retrieval system without written permission from the publisher

Table of Contents

Introduction

With their long limbs, prehensile tails, and quick movements across the forest canopy, spider monkeys are an amazing kind of monkey. We will dig into the fascinating world of spider monkeys in this thorough guide, examining their native environment, traits, behavior, and the factors to be taken into account when keeping them as pets.

The genus Ateles includes spider monkeys, which are endemic to the tropical jungles of Central and South America. Spider monkeys are known to exist in seven different species, each with distinct characteristics and geographic ranges. These species include, among others, the highly endangered black spider monkey, brown spider monkey, and black-headed spider monkey.

Spider monkeys are easily recognized by their long, thin limbs, which help them swing smoothly from branch to branch in the trees. Their prehensile tails, which have the ability to grasp items, act as an extra limb, giving them stability and making it easier for them to move around in their arboreal habitat.

Spider monkeys live mostly in the top canopy of tropical rainforests in the wild, where they eat a variety of plants and animals, including fruits, leaves, insects, and even small vertebrates. In addition to their nutrition, they have an amazing capacity to utilize a variety of food sources, which aids in their ability to adjust to environmental changes.

In terms of social organization, spider monkeys reside in sizable, mixed-gender groups that can have up to 30 members. Through grooming, vocalizations, and group activities like traveling and foraging, these groups have developed deep attachments that contribute to their high level of cohesiveness. There is a complicated social structure in these communities, with dominant members frequently controlling group dynamics and resources.

Spider monkeys are fascinating creatures, but they are threatened in the wild by a number of factors, such as habitat destruction, poaching, and the illicit pet trade. The International Union for Conservation of Nature (IUCN) has thus categorized a number of these species as endangered or critically endangered, underscoring the urgent need for conservation initiatives to save these recognizable primates and their delicate environments.

It is important for anyone thinking about owning a spider monkey as a pet to be aware of the challenges associated with providing for these creatures. Despite their adorable and playful appearance, spider monkeys have certain demands that call for their owners' constant attention and commitment. A strong commitment to the well-being and welfare of a spider monkey is necessary for appropriate ownership, ranging from providing enough space and enrichment to making sure they receive the right food and socializing.

We will go into great length on all the different facets of taking care of a spider monkey in the parts that follow in this guide, including housing needs, food and nutrition, medical attention, training, and safety concerns. A thorough study of these subjects will enable potential owners to make wise choices and provide their primate companion the best care possible.

Chapter 1

Legal Aspects and Licenses Associated with Keeping a Spider Monkey as a Pet

Keeping a spider monkey as a pet involves a lot of work and is subject to several rules and regulations. The keeping of exotic animals, such as spider monkeys, is governed by rules and regulations in many countries that are designed to safeguard the public and the animals themselves. We will look at the laws pertaining to owning spider monkeys in this part, as well as any necessary licenses and permissions.

- Comprehending Wildlife Laws:

It's important to get knowledgeable about local wildlife rules and restrictions before obtaining a spider monkey. These regulations can differ greatly between jurisdictions, and breaking them can have legal repercussions such as fines, the animal being seized, and even criminal charges.

- CITES Rules:

The Convention on International Trade in Endangered Species of Wild Fauna and Flora (CITES) is a global agreement that regulates the trade in threatened and endangered species, and it provides protection for spider monkeys. In order to guarantee that spider monkeys are acquired and traded lawfully and sustainably, permits and other paperwork are needed for the import, export, and exchange of spider monkeys and their parts.

- Federal Statutes:

Owning exotic animals, such as spider monkeys, is governed at the federal level in several nations. Certain rules may apply in a given nation to the ownership, breeding, and sale of exotic animals, including primates.

These regulations may mandate that, in order to protect the welfare of the animals, owners must apply for permits, submit to inspections, and follow particular care requirements.

- Laws of the State, Province, or Region:

The ownership of spider monkeys may be governed by state, provincial, or local laws that control the holding of exotic animals in addition to federal regulations. Depending on the area, these rules may differ greatly and include things like ownership limitations, housing standards, and permitting procedures. It is imperative that you investigate and abide by the particular laws that apply to your region.

- License and Permit Requirements:

It is often necessary to obtain a permit or license from the appropriate authorities in order to keep a spider monkey as a pet in many regions. Usually, departments or wildlife authorities in charge of controlling exotic animal ownership grant these permits. Providing thorough details regarding the intended enclosure, the animal's origins, and the owner's background and credentials may be required throughout the application process.

- Examining and Adhering to:

Wildlife officials may conduct inspections of spider monkey owners as part of the permitting procedure to make sure that the laws and standards of care are being followed. The effectiveness of the enclosure, the availability of appropriate food and enrichment, and the general health and welfare of the animal may all be the subject of an inspection. Revocation of the permit and other consequences could follow noncompliance with these requirements.

- Insurance and Liability:

There are risks associated with owning a spider monkey for both the public and the owner. It may be necessary for owners in certain jurisdictions to purchase liability insurance in order to guard against possible harm or damages brought on by the animal. In the event of an incident involving the spider monkey, this insurance may pay for medical costs, property damage, and legal fees.

- Moral Aspects to Take into Account:

In addition to the legal requirements, potential owners had to think about the moral ramifications of owning a spider monkey as a pet. Primates are sociable and highly cognitive creatures whose complex physical and psychological demands might be difficult to meet in a household environment. In addition to ensuring the animal's physical, mental, and emotional needs, responsible ownership entails honoring the animal's social structures and natural behaviors.

Managing a complicated legal environment that differs by jurisdiction is necessary while keeping a spider monkey as a pet. In addition to securing the required licenses or permits and making sure that welfare and care standards are followed, prospective owners must educate themselves on the rules and regulations that pertain to the ownership of exotic animals. Owners may preserve the wild populations of these amazing primates while simultaneously giving their companion a secure and rewarding living space by abiding by the law and moral principles.

Chapter 2

Spider monkey housing requirements: establishing a secure and stimulating environment

For a spider monkey to remain healthy, safe, and happy, they must have appropriate home. Spider monkeys are highly clever and active primates that need lots of room to roam around and investigate, as well as opportunities for socialization and cerebral stimulation. The housing needs for spider monkeys will be covered in detail in this extensive book, including with enclosure design, sizing concerns, environmental enrichment, and safety measures.

- Design of Enclosures:

It is essential to take into account the natural habits and habitat preferences of spider monkeys while creating enclosures for them. Because they are arboreal animals, spider monkeys spend most of their time in trees. As a result, the enclosure need to resemble a forest canopy with lots of vertical room for swinging and climbing.

- Inside Area:

The spider monkey should have plenty of space to walk around in the indoor section of the enclosure. It should be both large enough to support natural activities like jumping and swinging, as well as tall enough to support branches and other vertical climbing structures. The monkey should have access to platforms or shelves with different heights for resting spots and viewing positions within the enclosure.

- Outside Area:

Spider monkeys do best in outdoor habitats with access to a range of natural stimuli, natural sunlight, and fresh air. To keep monkeys inside and shield them from predators and trespassers, outdoor cages need to be impenetrably fenced. Additionally, to promote natural behaviors and physical activity, they ought to incorporate elements like trees, vines, and climbing structures.

- Climbing Frames and Contentment:

To keep spider monkeys mentally engaged and physically busy, enrichment is necessary. To promote activity and exploration, climbing frames, ropes, branches, and platforms ought to be arranged thoughtfully all throughout the enclosure. Toys, puzzle feeders, and foraging chances are further ways to reduce boredom and stop stereotypical behavior.

- Flooring and Substratum:

To give the spider monkey a cozy and secure surface, the substrate and flooring of the enclosure should be carefully chosen. Natural substrates that resemble the forest floor, such sand, mulch, or soil, enable foraging and digging activities. To maintain hygienic conditions and avoid accidents, non-toxic, easily cleaned flooring materials like rubber matting or artificial grass can also be utilized.

- Climate Control and Temperature:

Spider monkeys are exclusive to tropical rainforests, where they favor warm, humid climates. As a result, it's critical to keep the enclosure's temperature and humidity levels constant, particularly if the monkey will be living in an area with harsh seasonal variations or temperatures. It could be essential to install humidifiers or misters in addition to heating and cooling systems to provide the best possible atmosphere for the monkeys' comfort and well-being.

- Safety Measures:

When keeping a spider monkey, safety is of the utmost importance for both the pet and the people who look after them. To stop escape or harm, enclosures should be built with durable materials and firmly fastened. To reduce the likelihood of accidents or health issues, all potential hazards, such as sharp edges, poisonous plants, or small openings, should be eliminated or reduced.

- Getting Along and Socialization:

Being with their own kind, spider monkeys are gregarious creatures that enjoy each other's company. To encourage socialization and friendship, it is advised to place spider monkeys in harmonious groups wherever feasible. Nonetheless, to avoid disputes and guarantee the welfare of all participating monkeys, the introduction of new individuals should be carried out gradually and under the observation of knowledgeable caregivers.

It's important to carefully examine a spider monkey's natural activities, environment needs, and personal preferences while designing a suitable home for them. Owners may maintain the health and wellbeing of their pet spider monkey by providing a safe, stimulating environment that promotes social contact and natural activities. To further encourage physical and mental activity and avoid boredom or stress, routine upkeep, monitoring, and enrichment are crucial. Spider monkeys can have happy, meaningful lives in captivity when given the right care and attention to housing requirements, provided they are kept in a house with responsible and compassionate owners.

Chapter 3

Spider Monkey Nutrition & Diet: Fulfilling the Special Dietary Requirements of Primates

Ensuring the health and welfare of captive spider monkeys requires the provision of a well-rounded and nourishing food. Given their omnivorous nature, spider monkeys need a diverse diet that fulfills their individual nutritional needs. This diet should include a mix of fruits, vegetables, leafy greens, protein sources, and supplements. We will examine the nutritional requirements of spider monkeys in this extensive guide, along with suggested foods, feeding schedules, dietary supplements, and typical nutritional difficulties.

- Knowing the Nutrition of Spider Monkeys:

Spider monkeys are omnivores by nature, having evolved to eat a wide variety of fruits, leaves, flowers, insects, and occasionally small vertebrates. Fruits are the main source of energy and vital elements in their diet, which is rich in fiber, vitamins, and minerals.

- **Produce and Fruits:**

A spider monkey's diet should be based mostly on fresh fruits and vegetables because they are a good source of vitamins, minerals, and antioxidants. Fruits like bananas, apples, oranges, grapes, berries, melons, and tropical fruits like papaya, mango, and pineapple are frequently available. To add more nutrients and fiber, vegetables including bell peppers, cucumbers, squash, carrots, and leafy greens can be served.

- **Sources of Protein:**

Although their primary diet is fruit, spider monkeys also need protein for healthy growth of their muscles and tissues. In the wild, they eat insects, small animals, and sometimes even eggs or nestlings for nourishment.

Commercially produced monkey biscuits, boiled eggs, cooked lean meats (such chicken or turkey), mealworms, crickets, and other insect sources are some of the ways that protein can be given to animals kept in captivity.

- Vegetables and Forages:

Because they are an important source of vitamins, minerals, and fiber, leafy greens are an integral part of a spider monkey's diet. Kale, collard greens, spinach, dandelion greens, and bok choy are examples of regular offerings that can be given to enrich the monkey's diet and support good digestive health. Moreover, offering browse items like edible plants, branches, and leaves can promote natural foraging activities and stimulate the mind.

- Supplements for nutrition:

For spider monkeys, a diversified diet can supply the majority of critical elements; nonetheless, dietary supplements could be required to guarantee that all nutritional needs are satisfied. Supplements including calcium and vitamin D3 are very crucial for preserving bone health and preventing metabolic bone disease, especially in captive monkeys kept indoors. Depending on a person's demands and dietary inadequacies, other supplements including vitamin C, multivitamins, and omega-3 fatty acids could also be suggested.

- Mealtime Plans and Amounts:

It is important to feed spider monkeys several times a day to replicate their normal eating habits and avoid boredom or overindulgence. Larger meals are usually served in the morning and evening, with three to five small meals or snacks spread evenly throughout the day. To avoid obesity or malnutrition, portion sizes should be carefully monitored and modified based on the age, size, activity level, and general health status of the monkey.

- Drinking plenty of water

Sustaining good health and function in spider monkeys requires adequate water. There should always be access to fresh, clean water, supplied in bowls or bottles that are firmly fastened to the enclosure to avoid contamination or spills. Furthermore, providing meals high in water, including fruits and vegetables, can assist the monkey stay hydrated and avoid dehydration, particularly in warmer regions or during times when activity levels are higher.

- Observation and Modification:

To make sure that the spider monkeys' nutritional demands are being satisfied, it is crucial to regularly examine their diet, physical state, and general health. To spot any possible dietary deficits or health problems, owners should keep an eye on feeding habits, hunger, stool quality, and changes in weight or physical condition. Depending on personal preferences, dietary needs, and overall health, food modifications could be required; a veterinarian with experience caring for primates can provide guidance on this.

- Common Issues with Nutrition:

In captivity, spider monkeys may experience a number of nutritional difficulties, such as obesity, dental concerns, gastrointestinal disorders, and metabolic imbalances. These problems may be brought on by an inappropriate diet, overfeeding, a lack of variety in the diet, or insufficient availability to healthy foods. Owners need to be careful to keep an eye on their monkey's diet and consult a veterinarian if they have any worries about their general health or nutritional status.

Feeding spider monkeys in captivity a well-balanced and nutrient-rich food is crucial to their health and wellbeing. A wide variety of fruits, vegetables, protein sources, and vitamins can help owners make sure their monkey gets all the nutrition it needs to grow and thrive. Responsible nutrition management also includes adhering to a regular feeding schedule, keeping an eye on nutritional intake, and making necessary adjustments. Spider monkeys can live long, robust lives in captivity, displaying their natural habits and preserving their optimum health and vigor, provided they receive the right food and nutrients.

Chapter 4

Enrichment and Mental Stimulation for Captive Spider Monkeys: Fostering Adaptive Behaviors and Overall Welfare

Spider monkeys are highly clever and active primates that need opportunities to explore their surroundings, engage in natural activities, and exercise their cognitive talents. For this reason, enrichment and mental stimulation are essential components of their care. We will go over the value of enrichment for spider monkeys in this in-depth tutorial, along with a variety of enrichment tactics and strategies and useful advice for setting up a habitat that is both interesting and enriching for captive primates.

- Comprehending Enrichment

The term "enrichment" describes the supply of stimuli, activities, and surroundings that support the mental, emotional, and physical health of animals kept in captivity. As very bright and inquisitive animals, spider monkeys require enrichment to meet their inherent behavioral needs and avoid boredom and stress.

- Spider Monkeys' Behavioral Needs:

In the wild, spider monkeys engage in a variety of natural activities such as climbing, swinging, foraging, grooming, interacting with others, and investigating their environment. It is crucial to provide these behaviors opportunity in captivity in order to prevent stereotypical behaviors like pacing or self-harming behaviors and to enhance general well-being.

- Enhancement of the Environment:

The process of changing a monkey's living quarters to promote natural behaviors and offer chances for movement and exploration is known as environmental enrichment. To enable the monkeys to climb, swing, and jump, this can involve adding climbing frames, ropes, branches, platforms, and other elements that resemble the monkeys' natural habitat.

- Enhancement of Cognitive Function:

To maintain an active and engaged mind in a monkey, cognitive enrichment entails presenting challenges and mental stimulation. Puzzle feeders, foraging toys, scent trails, hidden goodies, and other activities that stimulate curiosity and problem-solving abilities can be examples of this.

- Enhancing Social Relations:

Being with their own kind, spider monkeys are gregarious creatures that enjoy each other's company. Giving monkeys the chance to socialize, communicate, and form bonds with other monkeys or similar species is known as social enrichment. Group living, watched playdates, grooming chances, and other socializing activities might all fall under this category.

- Freshness and Diverseness:

In order to keep the monkeys interested in enrichment activities and avoid them becoming habituated to them, it is imperative to introduce freshness and variation into their surroundings. This can be accomplished by adding fresh smells or textures, switching up the enclosure's arrangement, rotating the toys on a regular basis, and offering a variety of fresh foods.

- Enhancement of Senses:

Encouraging the monkey's five senses—sight, smell, touch, taste, and hearing—is known as sensory enrichment. Scent-infused items, sound-arousing ones, tactile materials, and visually engaging toys or décor can all help achieve this. Giving monkeys the chance to explore their senses can improve their overall sensory experience and improve their wellbeing.

- Instruction and Enhancement:

Given that it offers opportunities for positive reinforcement, cerebral stimulation, and physical exercise, training can be a beneficial kind of enrichment for spider monkeys. Teaching new behaviors, honing already acquired abilities, and fostering a bond of trust between the monkey and their caretakers are all possible goals of training sessions. One can employ positive reinforcement strategies to encourage the monkey and reinforce desired behaviors, including clicker training or food rewards.

- Complexity of the Environment:

To encourage natural behaviors and mental stimulation in spider monkeys, an environment that is rich and complicated is necessary. To promote exploration and provide monkeys the chance to exhibit their innate behaviors and preferences, enclosures should have a range of features, textures, heights, and hiding spots.

- Observation and Assessment:

Enrichment activities must be regularly observed and evaluated in order to determine their efficacy and make any necessary improvements. The best forms of enrichment for each particular monkey may be determined by keeping an eye on their behavior, degree of engagement, and general well-being.

To sum up, enrichment and mental stimulation are crucial parts of caring for spider monkeys since they encourage natural behaviors, lessen stress, and improve their general wellbeing in captivity. Owners may guarantee that their primate companion has a happy and satisfying life by creating an environment that is engaging and enriching that meets the monkey's physical, mental, and social needs. Additionally, to accommodate the monkey's evolving requirements and preferences and to support its long-term health and happiness, enrichment activities must be continuously observed, assessed, and adjusted.

Chapter 5

Veterinary and Health Care Requirements

In order to preserve the health and welfare of spider monkeys kept in captivity, proactive management and access to quality veterinary treatment are necessary. Spider monkeys can suffer from a wide range of health problems, including injuries, age-related ailments, dietary deficits, and infectious infections, much like any other animal. We will examine the medical needs and preventive care strategies for spider monkeys in this extensive guide, along with frequent ailments, veterinary exams, and emergency protocols.

- Preventive Medical Care:

Maintaining spider monkeys' general health and well-being and delaying the onset of disease require preventive healthcare. Preventive care comprises essential elements such as routine veterinarian exams, immunizations, dental care, parasite control, and diet management.

- Veterinary Exams:

Frequent veterinarian checks are necessary to track the health of spider monkeys and identify any possible problems before they become serious. The monkey's overall health, weight, body condition score, dental health, and vital signs will all be evaluated during a veterinarian examination. To check for underlying health issues, diagnostic procedures such as blood testing, fecal examinations, and others may be carried out.

- Immunizations:

Vaccinations are essential in preventing infectious diseases that could endanger the health of spider monkeys. Although there are no vaccinations created especially for spider monkeys, some may be suggested in light of the monkey's risk factors and exposure to particular illnesses. These could consist of immunizations against tetanus, rabies, and other zoonotic illnesses.

- Manage Parasites:

For spider monkeys, parasites including intestinal worms, fleas, ticks, and mites can be extremely harmful to their health. Consistent management of parasites, such as topical treatments and deworming drugs, is necessary to avoid infestations and preserve the health of the monkeys. Owners and their veterinarian should collaborate closely to create a parasite control plan that takes into account the unique requirements and risk factors of each monkey.

- Dental Health:

For spider monkeys, oral health is very important because tooth issues can result in pain, discomfort, and malnutrition. To stop dental disease and keep your mouth healthy, regular dental cleanings, exams, and brushings may be advised. Furthermore, encouraging natural chewing activity and preventing dental problems can be achieved by giving suitable chew toys and objects.

- Management of Nutrition:

Maintaining the health and vitality of spider monkeys requires proper nourishment. It's essential to provide a balanced diet that satisfies the unique nutritional needs of monkeys in order to prevent malnutrition, obesity, and associated health issues. To ensure that the monkey's diet is meeting its requirements, owners should collaborate closely with their veterinarian or a trained nutritionist for primates to create a plan that includes a range of fruits, vegetables, protein sources, and supplements.

- Typical Health Issues:

Numerous health difficulties, such as infectious diseases, malnutrition, dental problems, respiratory infections, gastrointestinal disorders, and musculoskeletal issues, can affect spider monkeys. The monkey's behavior, hunger, feces quality, and general health should all be closely observed by its owners for any indications of disease or pain. If there are any worries about the health of the monkey, they should be addressed by a veterinarian as once.

- Procedures for Emergencies:

It is crucial to have a strategy in place to guarantee the monkey receives timely and proper medical attention in the event of a medical emergency. Owners should be ready to take the monkey to a veterinarian clinic that is set up to handle exotic animals and should have access to a licensed veterinarian with experience caring for primates. Emergency supplies have to be easily accessible at all times, including first aid kits, prescription drugs, and contact details for veterinary specialists.

- Management of the Environment:

Spider monkeys' health and well-being can be greatly impacted by environmental elements as temperature, humidity, illumination, and ventilation. Enclosures must be kept at the proper humidity and temperature ranges for the species, have enough ventilation, and have access to either natural sunshine or artificial lighting. Maintaining the monkey's surroundings in a healthy state and stopping the development of infectious diseases also depend on cleanliness and hygiene.

- Observing Behavior:

Observing the behavior and social connections of the monkeys can reveal important information about their health and wellbeing. Behavior changes that include reduced activity, altered appetite, hostility, or social disengagement could be signs of underlying health issues or stressors that need to be addressed. Owners who have any worries about their monkey's behavior or mental health should pay close attention to these cues and consult a veterinarian.

Access to veterinary services and proactive health care are critical for maintaining the health and welfare of spider monkeys kept in captivity. Owners may assist their primate friend live a long and healthy life by instituting preventive care measures, keeping an eye on the monkey's health, and obtaining timely veterinarian intervention when necessary. In addition, giving spider monkeys a novel and enriching habitat, ensuring good nutrition, and fostering social interaction are crucial for preserving their general health and wellbeing.

Chapter 6

Instruction and Interaction

In order to foster positive social connections, cerebral stimulation, and trust between the monkey and their caretakers, training and socialization are crucial components of spider monkey care. By employing positive reinforcement methods and planned socializing activities, spider monkeys can form critical relationships, skills, and behaviors that improve their general well-being while living in captivity. We will examine the fundamentals of training and socializing for spider monkeys in this thorough book, as well as talk about training strategies and tactics and offer helpful advice for encouraging healthy social interactions and partnerships.

- Comprehending Socialization and Training:

Training entails using positive reinforcement strategies, like praise or rewards, to educate a spider monkey how to carry out particular actions or activities. Conversely, socialization entails giving the monkey chances to engage in constructive and regulated interactions with people or other monkeys of the same species. In order to encourage cerebral stimulation, lower stress levels, and foster strong interactions between the monkey and their caregivers, training and socializing are both crucial.

- Advantages of Socialization and Training:

For spider monkeys, socialization and training have several advantages, such as:

Mental Stimulation: By giving monkeys opportunities for problem-solving, exploration, and cognitive enrichment, training and socialization activities help to keep their minds sharp and occupied.

Building Trust: Training facilitates easier handling, medical treatments, and husbandry operations by fostering positive relationships and trust between the monkey and its caregivers.

Environmental enrichment takes the form of training and socializing activities, which give the monkey chances for exercise, social connection, and mental stimulation.

Behavioral management: By encouraging positive behaviors and rerouting bad ones, training can assist in addressing unwanted tendencies like fearfulness, anger, or stereotyping.

Communication: Training makes it easier for the monkey and their caretakers to communicate, which promotes collaboration and improved understanding in a variety of settings.

- Training using Positive Reinforcement:

For teaching spider monkeys new behaviors and rewarding desired behaviors, positive reinforcement training is a popular and successful technique. With this approach, the monkey is more likely to repeat the intended behavior in the future when they get food, praise, or other positive stimuli as rewards for carrying out the task.

- Methods of Training:

Spider monkeys can be trained to learn new behaviors and modify their current ones using a variety of training methods. Among these methods are:

Target training involves teaching a monkey to follow or touch a target—a stick or other hand-held object, for example—in order to lead them into desirable positions or actions.

Shaping: Using a series of approximations to gradually shape a complex behavior by breaking it down into smaller, more manageable steps.

Capturing: Rewarding the monkey for performing the desired behavior on its own when it happens naturally.

Desensitization and counterconditioning: To modify the monkey's emotional reaction, progressively expose it to stimuli that cause fear or anxiety while associating those stimuli with pleasant memories or rewards.

- Training Objectives and Conduct:

Spider monkey training objectives might change based on the needs, preferences, and situations of each individual. Spider monkeys frequently engage in the following training activities:

Teaching a monkey to touch something with their nose or hand so they can move and manipulate it more easily is known as target training.

Teaching a monkey to stay in a specific location, or station, while receiving medical attention, grooming, or feeding.

Teaching the monkey to willingly engage in husbandry tasks, such showing body parts for inspection, taking medicine, or letting nails be clipped, is known as husbandry behavior.

Teaching the monkey to participate in enrichment activities—like puzzle feeders, foraging missions, or interactive toys—is known as enrichment behavior.

Social behaviors: Encouraging the monkey to engage in healthy social interactions with humans or other monkeys through group activities, supervised play sessions, and grooming chances.

- Opportunities for Socialization:

Giving a monkey the chance to socialize with humans, other animals, or conspecifics in a constructive and regulated way is known as socialization. In addition to lowering stress and promoting social behaviors that spider monkeys naturally exhibit, socialization can help build healthy relationships.

Group Housing: Individual spider monkeys can naturally interact, communicate, and form bonds with one another when they are housed in appropriate groups. Care should be taken while managing group housing to avoid conflicts and guarantee the welfare of all participating monkeys.

Supervised Play Sessions: In a controlled setting, supervised play sessions enable spider monkeys to communicate, play, and engage in social interactions with other animals or conspecifics. Playdates should be watched over to avoid violence or accidents and to encourage healthy sociability.

Human Interaction: Trust and good connections with spider monkeys are developed through positive encounters with humans. Through training sessions, social bonding chances, enrichment activities, and grooming, caregivers should spend time interacting with the monkey.

Environmental Enrichment: Activities that foster social connection, including shared playthings, cooperative chores, or group feeding, can foster cooperation and social bonding amongst spider monkeys living in the same home.

- Developing a Close Bond and Trust:

With spider monkeys, it takes time, patience, consistency, and positive reinforcement to establish trust and healthy relationships. When interacting with the monkey, caregivers should maintain composure and show respect. They should also handle the animal gently and give praise or rewards for desired behaviors. Positive and cooperative interactions gradually increase when a monkey is treated consistently and predictably, as this fosters trust and confidence in the animal.

- Observation and Assessment:

To determine their efficacy and make any modifications, training and socialization programs must be regularly observed and evaluated. Training methods can be improved and problem areas can be found by keeping an eye on the monkey's behavior, degree of involvement, and reaction to cues. Consulting with seasoned trainers, behaviorists, or veterinarians can offer insightful advice on how to handle difficult training situations or behavioral issues.

Socialization and training are crucial aspects of caring for spider monkeys since they foster mental development, the establishment of trust, and fruitful social relationships while they are in captivity. In a captive setting, spider monkeys can flourish and display their natural behaviors by employing positive reinforcement strategies, offering socialization chances, and cultivating healthy connections with caregivers. Additionally, to accommodate the monkey's evolving requirements and preferences and to support its long-term health and well-being, continual observation, assessment, and modification of training and socializing activities are required.

Chapter 7

Safety Measures to Take While Taking Care of Spider Monkeys for Owners and Visitors

When taking care of these clever and nimble primates, it is crucial to ensure the safety of both humans and spider monkeys. Because of their unique physical and behavioral traits, spider monkeys should be handled carefully to avoid mishaps, injuries, and disputes. This thorough tutorial will go over how to interact with spider monkeys safely for both owners and visitors. It will cover handling techniques, enclosure design, visiting guidelines, and emergency protocols.

- Designing and maintaining enclosures:

Ensuring the safety of both people and spider monkeys is contingent upon the design and upkeep of the cage. Important things to think about are:

Secure Fencing: To stop intruders or predators from escaping or gaining unauthorized entrance, the enclosure needs to be securely fenced. The height of the fencing should deter monkeys from climbing over it, and it should be made of sturdy materials that are difficult for them to break through.

Structure of Enclosure: The enclosure should be free of potential risks, sharp edges, and protrusions that could injure humans or monkeys. It should also be structurally sound. To find and fix any structural problems quickly, routine maintenance and inspections are crucial.

Preventing the monkey from escaping can be achieved by taking precautions like locking doors, windows, and other such openings. To stop unauthorized people from entering the enclosure, locks, latches, and other security measures should be employed.

Hazard Removal: Eliminate anything that could endanger the monkey or people from the enclosure, including any poisonous plants, sharp objects, electrical cords, or tiny gaps. Check the enclosure frequently for dangers, and take necessary action to eliminate or lessen them.

- Guidelines for Handling and Interaction:

It is crucial to use the right handling methods and protocols while engaging with spider monkeys in order to avoid mishaps and reduce the monkeys' stress. Important things to think about are:

Respect Personal Space: Stay out of the monkey's way and let them come to you when they're ready. The monkey may become frightened or startled by abrupt movements or gestures, which could result in aggressive or protective actions.

Steer clear of Direct Eye Contact: Spider monkeys may react aggressively or defensively if they perceive direct eye contact as a danger or challenge. Rather, keep your posture relaxed and refrain from looking the monkey in the eye.

Gentle Handling: Avoid grasping or securing the monkey with force; instead, handle them slowly and gently. Steadily support the monkey's body, taking care not to push on delicate parts like the limbs or abdomen.

Oversee Interactions: To guarantee appropriate and safe conduct, oversee interactions between the monkey and other people, particularly young ones. Inform visitors on appropriate ways to interact with the monkeys and the value of honoring their limits.

Refrain from Feeding by Hand: To avoid unintentional bites or injury, refrain from feeding spider monkeys by hand. Instead, provide food in a controlled and safe manner by using enrichment devices or feeding stations.

- Guidelines & Instructions for Visitors:

To protect both the visitors' safety and the monkeys' wellbeing, it is crucial to provide clear instructions and education while hosting visitors or guests at a facility housing spider monkeys. Important things to think about are:

Educate Visitors: Before allowing visitors to enter the enclosure, provide them information on safety precautions, suitable interaction tactics, and spider monkey behavior. Encourage visitors who are unsure about appropriate behavior to ask questions and seek advice from staff members.

Visitor Supervision: Make sure that guests visiting the spider monkey enclosure are under the guidance of informed staff members or guides who are able to keep an eye on interactions, respond to inquiries, and step in if needed to stop dangerous conduct.

Limit Access: To prevent unwanted entry and protect the safety of both visitors and the monkeys, limit access to specific portions of the enclosure or facility. Utilize staff supervision, signage, and obstacles to manage guest access and avert mishaps or disputes.

Provide Handwashing Stations: To promote good hygiene habits and lower the danger of disease transmission between humans and monkeys, place handwashing or hand sanitizer stations next to the spider monkey cage.

- Plans for contingencies and emergency procedures:

When taking care of spider monkeys, mishaps or emergencies can still happen. To react swiftly and efficiently to any circumstance, emergency protocols and backup plans must be in place. Important things to think about are:

Veterinary professionals, animal control officials, and other pertinent individuals who can help in an emergency should all have their emergency contact information listed.

First Aid Supplies: Always have a fully supplied first aid kit on hand, complete with items for treating small wounds and doing basic first treatment. Make sure that employees are knowledgeable about common injuries and medical situations and have received first aid training.

Establish evacuation protocols to ensure the safe removal of both humans and monkeys from the enclosure in the event of a fire, natural disaster, or other emergency. Regularly practice evacuation exercises to make that staff members are equipped to act promptly and effectively in an emergency.

Animal restraint tools: Keep the right tools on hand, such as nets, poles, or capture cages, to securely capture and confine monkeys when needed. Make certain that employees are properly trained to operate this equipment and are aware of the safe and humane ways to handle monkeys.

- Frequent Reviews of Safety and Training:

Sustaining a safe and secure environment for humans and spider monkeys requires regular safety inspections and ongoing training. Important things to think about are:

Employee Education: Conduct frequent training courses on spider monkey behavior, handling methods, safety measures, and emergency protocols for employees. Make certain that employees are competent and self-assured in their capacity to tend to the monkeys and handle emergencies.

Safety Audits: To find any possible risks or safety issues, conduct routine safety audits of the facility and the enclosure housing the spider monkeys. To avoid mishaps or injuries, take immediate action to resolve any problems and put corrective measures in place.

Establish protocols for reporting and recording mishaps, near-misses, and occurrences involving humans or spider monkeys. To lower the chance of recurrence, look into the underlying reasons of accidents and put preventative measures in place.

In conclusion, when taking care of these sharp-witted and nimble primates, safety measures are critical to guaranteeing both the wellbeing of spider monkeys and people. A safe and secure habitat where spider monkeys can flourish and have pleasant connections with humans can be created by owners and caretakers by adhering to appropriate cage design, handling techniques, visitor guidelines, and emergency procedures. Maintaining a culture of safety and averting mishaps or events in the future also requires continual training, instruction, and safety reviews.

Chapter 8

Typical Obstacles and Problem Solving

The obstacles of caring for spider monkeys in captivity are diverse and include social dynamics, environmental factors, behavioral problems, and health issues. For the sake of these socially adept and clever primates, it is imperative that these issues be recognized and resolved quickly. In this thorough guide, we will examine some typical problems that arise when taking care of spider monkeys and offer helpful advice and methods to assist resolve them.

Conduct Issues:

a. hostility:

Aggression against people or conspecifics can be exhibited by spider monkeys for a number of reasons, such as dominance, fear, stress, or territoriality. To deal with hostility:

1. Determine the root cause of aggressiveness and deal with any social or environmental pressures.
2. Use training methods based on positive reinforcement to curb aggressive conduct and encourage constructive interactions.
3. Give the monkey the chance to exhibit his or her normal actions in order to relieve boredom or irritation.
4. For individualized advice and assistance, speak with a licensed veterinarian or animal behaviorist who specializes in primate behavior.

b. Stereotypical Actions:

Stress, boredom, or a lack of environmental stimulation can lead to the development of stereotypical behaviors in captive spider monkeys, such as pacing, self-harming actions, or repetitive motions. In order to combat stereotyped actions:

1. Determine the underlying stressors or environmental deficits that may be causing the behavior, then take appropriate action.
2. Use techniques for environmental enrichment to stimulate the mind and promote organic behaviors.
3. To relieve boredom and lower stress, offer opportunities for social connection, physical activity, and cognitive enrichment.
4. If stereotypical behaviors don't go away or get worse in spite of intervention efforts, keep a close eye on the monkey's behavior and consult a veterinarian.

Health Issues:

a. Inadequate Dietary Resources:

In captivity, nutritional deficits in spider monkeys can occur, particularly if their diet is deficient in important vitamins or minerals. To remedy dietary inadequacies:

1. To make sure the monkeys' diet satisfies their unique nutritional needs, review and modify it.

2. For individualized nutritional advice and supplements, if needed, speak with a licensed veterinarian or primate nutritionist.

3. To spot and treat any indications of malnutrition or health problems connected to deficiencies, keep a close eye on the monkey's weight, appetite, and general well-being.

b. Diseases Caused by Infections:

Viral, bacterial, and parasitic illnesses are among the many infectious disorders that spider monkeys are prone to. In order to control and avoid infectious diseases:

1. Adopt stringent biosecurity measures to stop viruses from entering and spreading throughout the monkey population.
2. Vaccinate the monkeys against prevalent infectious diseases in accordance with the advice of a licensed veterinarian.
3. To keep an eye out for symptoms of illness and infection, perform routine health screenings such as physical examinations, fecal examinations, and blood testing.
4. To stop the transmission of infectious diseases, isolate newcomers and thoroughly examine them before integrating them into the community of habituated primates.

Environmental Difficulties:

a. Poor Design of Enclosure:

Inadequate enclosure design has the potential to exacerbate behavioral problems, stress, and boredom in spider monkeys. In order to address the poor enclosure design:

1. Examine the enclosure's size, features, and arrangement at the moment to find any shortcomings or potential improvements.
2. Make necessary changes to the enclosure to better suit the monkey's demands, such as adding more room for climbing, swinging, and exploration.
3. To make the environment more engaging and enriching, include naturalistic features like trees, branches, and hiding places.
4. Follow routine maintenance and cleaning procedures to keep the enclosure aesthetically pleasing, hygienic, and safe.

b. Climate Control and Temperature:

For spider monkeys to remain healthy and happy, the right temperature and humidity levels must be maintained, particularly in areas with harsh weather. To solve problems with climate control and temperature:

1. Install air conditioning and heating units in the enclosure to keep the temperature there comfortable all year round.
2. To make sure that the temperature and humidity levels stay within the ideal range for spider monkeys, frequently check them and make any necessary adjustments.
3. Give the monkeys access to airflow, shade, and cover so they may control their body temperature naturally.
4. To modify humidity levels and provide the monkeys with a more pleasant atmosphere, think about utilizing fans, humidifiers, or misters.

Social Difficulties:

a. Social Structure and Disagreement:

Within their intricately structured social groups, which have well-defined hierarchies, spider monkeys are known to engage in intragroup fights.

To deal with conflict and social hierarchy:

1. Keep a close eye on social interactions and step in when necessary to stop bullying or acts of aggression.
2. Give the monkeys opportunities for play, grooming, and cooperative activities to help them form and preserve social bonds.
3. Make sure that the dynamics within the group are stable and harmonious, and if conflicts arise or intensify, think about separating people.

4. Use training methods based on positive reinforcement to strengthen social ties within the group and encourage cooperative behavior.

b. Social Detachment:

Given that spider monkeys are gregarious creatures who benefit from social engagement, social isolation may have unfavorable effects on them. In order to combat social isolation:

1. Make sure the groups of spider monkeys in your care are compatible and provide them with opportunities for companionship and social contact.

2. Offer enrichment activities, such group feeding, grooming sessions, and cooperative play, that promote social connection.

3. Keep an eye on the dynamics between the group's members and take action if anyone exhibits symptoms of social exclusion or isolation.

4. To minimize friction and promote social group integration, think about acclimating new members gradually.

Challenges in Training and Enrichment:

a. Absence of Motivation or Engagement:

During training or enrichment activities, spider monkeys may show signs of low engagement or motivation, particularly if they grow bored or uninterested. To overcome a deficiency in motivation or engagement:

1. Regularly switch up the training and enrichment activities to keep the monkeys interested and active.

2. To boost incentive and excitement for attending training sessions, use high-value prizes and positive reinforcement strategies.

3. Adjust training and enrichment activities to the specific likes and skills of each monkey, including things that fit with their innate interests and behaviors.

4. To keep the monkeys interested and motivated, keep an eye on how they react to training and enrichment activities and modify the strategy as necessary.

b. Training Difficulties:

Spider monkeys are intelligent, agile, and have a strong sense of will, which makes training them difficult. To deal with difficulties in training:

1. Divide training assignments into more manageable, smaller steps, and progressively advance the monkey's learning curve.

2. To promote collaboration and reinforce desired behaviors, use positive reinforcement strategies like praise or awards.

3. When training, exercise patience, consistency, and persistence. Refrain from utilizing harsh punishment or approaches that could incite resistance or tension.

4. Seek advice from seasoned behaviorists or trainers who specialize in dealing with monkeys and can offer tailored counsel and support.

Managing typical problems in the care of spider monkeys necessitates a proactive, multidimensional strategy that takes into account the special requirements and traits of these social, intelligent primates. Spider monkeys in captivity can be kept happy and healthy provided owners and caregivers recognize and swiftly treat behavioral, health, environmental, social, and training issues. Maintaining a secure, engaging, and rewarding environment where spider monkeys can flourish and lead fulfilling lives also requires constant observation, assessment, and modification of management techniques.

Chapter 9

Conscientious Ownership and Moral Issues

It is extremely important to maintain ethical standards, look out for the wellbeing of your spider monkeys, and work toward their conservation—both in the wild and in captivity. Responsible ownership include giving the monkeys the proper attention, acknowledging their needs and natural habits, and actively participating in conservation initiatives to save their natural habitats and populations. This thorough handbook will cover the fundamentals of ethical ownership and responsible spider monkey care, including welfare concerns, conservation implications, legal requirements, and moral conundrums.

- Welfare Aspects to Take into Account:

a. Nutrition and Physical Well-Being:

It is necessary to provide the fundamental physical needs of spider monkeys, such as giving them access to wholesome food, clean water, suitable housing, and veterinary treatment, as part of responsible ownership. Owners are responsible for making sure the monkeys get a nutritious, well-balanced diet, frequent checkups, and timely care for any wounds or illnesses.

b. Mental Health:

Spider monkeys are gregarious and highly intellectual primates who need mental exercise, social contact, and chances to engage in their natural behaviors in order to be psychologically healthy. It is the responsibility of responsible owners to offer their monkeys exciting activities, interaction chances, and enrichment activities so that they can exhibit their natural behaviors without being bored or stressed.

c. Enhancement of the Environment:

Enhancing the psychological well-being of cage spider monkeys requires environmental enrichment. To maintain the monkeys' mental, physical, and emotional fulfillment, owners should offer a range of enrichment activities, including climbing structures, foraging opportunities, puzzle feeders, and social interactions.

d. Veterinary Treatment and Health Surveillance:

For spider monkeys to have any health problems identified and treated, routine veterinary treatment and health monitoring are essential. Appropriate owners should schedule routine checkups with a licensed veterinarian with experience caring for primates, as well as swiftly handle any emerging medical problems or emergencies.

e. Social Engagement and Creating Bonds:

Spider monkeys are gregarious primates that develop close relationships with both their group members and caretakers. In order to improve the bond between the monkeys and their human caretakers and foster a sense of security and trust, conscientious owners should offer their monkeys opportunities for social interaction, bonding, and positive reinforcement training.

- Implications for Conservation:

a. Breeding in captivity and managing the population:

A responsible approach to owning spider monkeys is taking into account the wider conservation consequences of captive breeding and population control. While refraining from actions that can encourage overbreeding or the exploitation of the species, owners should support moral breeding initiatives that place a high priority on genetic variety, species conservation, and long-term viability.

b. Knowledge and Consciousness:

As spokesman for their species, spider monkeys promote the value of environmental preservation and primate conservation. The public should be informed about spider monkeys, their natural history, risks to conservation, and the value of protecting their native habitats and ecosystems by responsible owners using their platform.

c. Endorsing Environmental Initiatives:

Owners who practice responsible behavior should actively support organizations and conservation efforts aimed at preserving the habitats and species of spider monkeys. This could be making donations to conservation initiatives, taking part in fundraising activities, volunteering for fieldwork or conservation projects, and supporting laws that support the preservation of natural habitats.

d. Ecological Methods:

Adopting sustainable techniques to reduce the environmental impact of caring for spider monkeys is a fundamental component of responsible ownership. Using environmentally friendly items, cutting back on waste and energy use, and encouraging sustainable forestry and agriculture methods can all contribute to preserving the natural habitats of species, including spider monkeys.

- Legal Requirements:

a. Required Permits:

Owning spider monkeys may be governed by laws and require a permit, depending on the jurisdiction. A responsible owner should become informed with local laws and rules pertaining to the ownership and upkeep of spider monkeys, secure any licenses or permits that may be required, and observe all other legal requirements pertaining to the ownership of primates.

b. Welfare Levels:

Welfare standards and regulations are in place in many nations and jurisdictions to guarantee the humane treatment and care of captive animals, including spider monkeys. In addition to providing suitable shelter, food, and medical attention, conscientious owners ought to uphold these welfare standards and take proactive steps to enhance their monkeys' quality of life.

c. Regulations on Import and Export:

Regulations pertaining to import and export may apply to spider monkeys traveling across international borders. It is imperative for conscientious owners to adhere to all relevant import and export regulations, secure any required licenses or certifications, and guarantee that the monkeys are handled with utmost care and safety, following global standards and optimal methodologies.

- Moral Conundrums:

a. Placement in a Sanctuary vs. Private Ownership:
One moral conundrum that proprietors of spider monkeys face is deciding whether to keep their pets in their homes or send them to sanctuaries or other approved establishments. While some monkey owners may give their monkeys exceptional care and enrichment, others might not have the means or know-how to sufficiently meet their demands. When making decisions concerning the care and placement of their monkeys, conscientious owners ought to take into account what's best for the animals and consult with knowledgeable specialists.

b. Breeding for Captive Welfare vs. Conservation Breeding:

Ensuring the safety and well-being of individuals in captivity while simultaneously breeding spider monkeys for conservation purposes presents another ethical conundrum. Programs for captive breeding monkeys must put the health, welfare, and moral treatment of the participating monkeys first, even though they may be essential to the conservation of the species. Owners who practice responsibility ought to back breeding initiatives that uphold moral and welfare norms and put the welfare of the monkeys first.

c. Public Exhibition and Instruction:

In order to promote awareness of their species and conservation issues, spider monkeys are frequently displayed in zoos, wildlife parks, and educational institutions. Public displays have the potential to create ethical questions regarding the health and well-being of the monkeys, even though they can also serve to inform and motivate people to care about wildlife. The health and happiness of the monkeys should come first for conscientious owners, who should make sure the facilities meet or beyond welfare standards and offer opportunities for interaction and enrichment.

- Appropriate Ownership Techniques:

a. Education and Research:

Before obtaining a spider monkey, conscientious owners should educate and research the species thoroughly, learning about its natural history, care needs, and current state of conservation. This entails being aware of the social, behavioral, and environmental requirements of spider monkeys and making sure that they are able to give the monkeys the proper attention and enrichment throughout their life.

b. Dedicated to Enduring Care:

Given that they can survive for several decades in captivity, spider monkeys need their owners to make a long-term commitment to them. In addition to satisfying their physical, social, and psychological needs, conscientious owners should be ready to offer their monkeys with lifelong care that adjusts as the animals become older and their needs change.

c. Working together and establishing connections:

Collaborating with other owners, caretakers, veterinarians, researchers, and conservationists to exchange information, resources, and best practices for maintaining spider monkeys is an integral part of responsible ownership. Building relationships with other ape community stakeholders can be a great way to get advice, possibilities for cooperation, and support for the conservation and well-being of spider monkeys.

d. Outreach and Advocacy:

By means of outreach, education, and public engagement initiatives, conscientious owners ought to promote the well-being and preservation of spider monkeys. This could entail promoting ethical ownership behaviors both within and outside of the primate community, supporting conservation efforts, and increasing public knowledge of the dangers facing spider monkeys and their ecosystems.

In conclusion, caring for a spider monkey's physical, social, and psychological requirements, promoting its conservation, and maintaining moral guidelines for handling and caring for them are all necessary for responsible spider monkey ownership. By putting spider monkeys' happiness and well-being first, honoring their natural habitats and behaviors, and abiding by the law

Chapter 10

Frequently Asked Questions (FAQs) about Owning and Caring for Spider Monkeys

Many people who are interested in animals find spider monkeys to be fascinating and intelligent primates. But there are certain difficulties and things to think about when owning and taking care of these unusual creatures. This thorough guide will answer many of the most common questions (FAQs) about owning and caring for spider monkeys, offering professional direction and advice to assist both new and seasoned owners in navigating the challenges of taking care of these amazing animals.

- Can people own spider monkeys as pets?

Spider monkeys are clever, highly social primates with intricate behavioral, social, and environmental requirements. Even though they could be fascinating animals, it is not morally or practically acceptable to keep them as pets. Large, naturalistic enclosures, specialized foods, and social interaction with conspecifics are all necessary for the survival of spider monkeys and are difficult, if not impossible, to provide in a conventional household. Furthermore, owning pet spider monkeys could support the illicit wildlife trade and the exploitation of these threatened species.

- What legal prerequisites must one meet in order to own a spider monkey?

Depending on the jurisdiction, possessing a spider monkey may entail obtaining licenses, permits, and compliance with rules on the ownership and upkeep of exotic animals. Because of welfare and conservation concerns, possessing spider monkeys may be strictly regulated or outlawed in many nations and regions. Before purchasing a spider monkey, potential owners should familiarize themselves with the rules and legislation pertaining to the ownership of primates in their community and secure any required licenses or permissions.

- Does the spider monkey require a lot of space?

Because they are arboreal creatures, spider monkeys need lots of room to climb, swing, and explore. Spider monkeys kept in captivity must to be kept in spacious, realistic enclosures that replicate their native surroundings and offer chances for exercise and environmental enrichment. A minimum of several hundred square meters of outdoor area per monkey is advised, while the exact size of the enclosure will depend on the number of monkeys and each one's unique needs.

- What nourish spider monkeys?

Although their primary diet is fruit, spider monkeys also eat a range of other plant items such as leaves, seeds, flowers, and insects. This means that they are largely frugivorous. Spider monkeys kept in captivity should be provided a well-balanced diet that satisfies their nutritional needs and mimics their natural eating patterns. A range of fruits, vegetables, leafy greens, nuts, seeds, and protein sources like eggs or insects may be included in this. To create a meal plan customized to the individual requirements of the monkeys, it is imperative to confer with a trained veterinarian or nutritionist specializing in primates.

- Do spider monkeys have an aggressive nature?

Although spider monkeys are generally not hostile toward humans, there are times when they might act aggressively, such as when they feel cornered, threatened, or stressed. In social groups of spider monkeys, aggression can also arise between individuals, particularly during mating season or while building dominance hierarchies. Spider monkey aggression can be reduced with careful handling, socialization, and environmental enrichment, but caution and respect for the monkey's limits are necessary in all encounters.

- What is the lifespan of spider monkeys?

Spider monkeys can live for several decades in captivity; their lifespans can be as long as twenty to thirty years. A spider monkey's exact lifespan is determined by a number of variables, including as environment, diet, veterinary care, and genetics. When thinking about caring for and owning a spider monkey, responsible owners should be ready to make a long-term commitment because these animals need constant care and attention to maintain their health and well-being.

- Are spider monkeys suitable as pets?

Because of their complicated social needs, long-term commitment, and particular care requirements, spider monkeys are not recommended as pets for most people. Spider monkey pet ownership can be difficult, costly, and even detrimental to the welfare of the monkeys. Additionally, due to welfare and conservation concerns, possessing spider monkeys may be prohibited or heavily regulated in many places. Those who are interested in spider monkeys are urged to volunteer at primate sanctuaries, support conservation initiatives, or pursue jobs in wildlife conservation and study as opposed to owning them as pets.

- What can I do to support the wild survival of spider monkeys?

Supporting the preservation of spider monkeys and their natural environments can be done in a variety of ways. Among the things people can do are:

1. providing financial support, volunteer labor, or fundraising efforts to respectable conservation groups that defend spider monkeys and their habitats.

2. increasing public knowledge of the dangers that spider monkeys face, including habitat loss, deforestation, and the illicit wildlife trafficking, via means of outreach, advocacy, and educational programs.

3. encouraging eco-friendly and sustainable activities, such as lowering carbon emissions, boosting responsible tourism, and supporting

sustainable agriculture, that contribute to the preservation of spider monkeys' and other species' natural habitats.

4. spreading knowledge among people about the value of preserving biodiversity and the interdependence of all living things in ecosystems.

- What moral issues arise from having a spider monkey as a pet?

Having a spider monkey brings up moral questions about responsible stewardship, conservation, and animal care. Important ethical factors to think about include:

1. ensuring the monkeys' physical and mental health through appropriate care, stimulation, and interaction.

2. encouraging local and international conservation initiatives to save spider monkeys and their natural environments.

3. giving spider monkeys the chance to exhibit their traits as members of their species while also honoring their natural demands and habits.

4. advocating for laws and procedures that address the root causes of animal exploitation and habitat loss as well as the humane treatment and care of captive primates.

- In the wild, what should I do if I come across a spider monkey?

It's important to keep your distance and refrain from bothering or approaching a spider monkey you come across in the wild. Being wild creatures, spider monkeys can become defensive or wary if they sense danger or are cornered. The following recommendations will help you interact with spider monkeys in the wild:

Keep a safe distance from the spider monkey to prevent tension or excitement. This is a sign of respect. To study the monkey from a distance without encroaching on its territory, use binoculars or a zoom lens on your camera.

Steer clear of abrupt movements and loud noises: Spider monkeys might be startled or scared by sudden movements and loud noises. To prevent frightening the monkey and making it run away or become defensive, move gently and softly.

Avoid trying to feed or handle the monkey: Feeding wild animals can cause behavioral disruptions and make them dependent on human assistance. The potential of fights or injury increases when spider monkeys become accustomed to human presence, so avoid giving them food or trying to touch or engage with them.

Spider monkeys need intact forests for food, housing, and protection, so please be mindful of their habitat. By staying on authorized pathways, avoiding trampling vegetation, and reducing your environmental effect, you can show respect for their ecosystem. Avoid disturbing spider monkeys' nests, feeding areas, or other vital supplies.

Silently and responsibly observe: Spend some time watching spider monkeys in their natural environment, taking in their grace and manners from a respectful distance. To get a closer look without encroaching on their personal space and without interfering with their social connections or activities, use binoculars or a spotting scope.

Report any unlawful activity: Notify local authorities or conservation organizations right away if you come across any illegal activity, such as poaching, habitat degradation, or wildlife trafficking. You can aid in the conservation efforts and prevent further harm to spider monkeys and their habitats by reporting unlawful activity.

You may contribute to ensuring spider monkeys' welfare and protection in the wild by adhering to these rules and respecting their natural activities and habitats. Recall that wild animals should not be kept as pets or exposed to human meddling; instead, they should be watched from a distance and enjoyed in their natural habitat.

www.ingramcontent.com/pod-product-compliance
Lightning Source LLC
Chambersburg PA
CBHW050814250726
48653CB00006B/2212